Poetry in Eden

FELICIA IYAMU

Poetry in Eden

FELICIA IYAMU

DEDICATION

It is about time we got out of this place and
It is about time we let go of it all.
And it is good we acknowledge the reality of it all too.
Bad timing can ruin anything,
But, really, there is no such thing.
Yes, it is pure bliss when we get down off
The jagged hill of life,
Through the leaking tunnels,
Around the Nessie Lake,
And move towards the bright shining sun
To find ourselves again.
Just remember to keep your eyes on the road.

The rear-view is not the main view, my friend.

This book is dedicated to all the wanderers;
To all the pure hearted souls;
To all the misfits and the 'degenerates.'
This book is dedicated to the 'crazy ones;'
To the curious, open minded, spiritual ones.
To the people like my mother, Jacqueline Ann McKenzie,
Who loved with all her heart —

Who become light beams into infinity
On this precious earth.

Yes, into infinity
Where there are limitless possibilities . . .
This one is for you.

POETRY IN EDEN

is a part of the author's broader mission to
uncover the universal human search for meaning
through philosophy and poetry,
while raising awareness about healing generational
trauma via geopolitical and historical research.

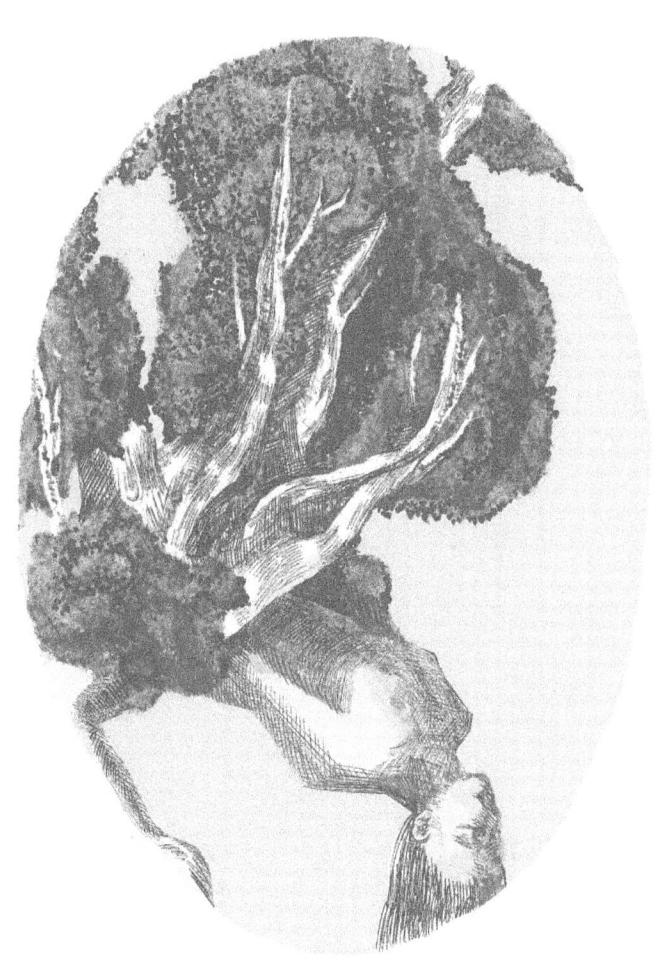

EARTH

I AM THE PORTAL

I am the portal
To the Earth and the land we walk on.
Yes, it is here among the pestilence
Where the feeling of home is closest to me
Because you see, this dear life
Means the world to me.

I am the portal
To the Earth and the land we walk on.
She parts the seas to the shore
So we can explore and uncover
Who and where we are meant to be.
Yes, who and where we are meant to be.

We are the portal
To the Earth and the land we walk on.
To the hole in the sea which
Opens to our shared destiny.
We all deserve to be free. Yes,
We all deserve to be free.

Here in Eden
There is no reason
To fear an ultimate unity.
Yes, here in Eden
We find communion
In all the things that make us . . . We.

PEACE'S FREQUENCY

I lie on my back. I feel at peace. The ceilings are high, and the room is filled with smoke from Nepalese incense. I spread my arms out like a cross. "I surrender," I whisper to the Gods.

My spine contorts, my hands and feet support my levitation. My meditation has brought me closer to Jah. Baptised at sunset, the roots of a tree come out of me, below me into the earth. And through my stomach, my womb and navel become stable for the trunks of this tree.

The tree is growing up, green and lush, branches bending before my eyes. I let out a sigh. The birth of a tree vertically as I lay horizontally. What a sight to see.

But, the tree does not stop. It reaches high, high up into the heavens. A hand reaches down. It is so profound. A gesture of the best type of union. It is a holy communion with Allah.

I am thankful. I am grateful. I vibrate at peace's frequency. God chose me to birth this tree. Yes, God chose me to birth this tree! This tree will see everything!

REBIRTH

I carry your dreams with me.
Then they take longer to return
To the Earth — for what it is worth
It is all a divine cycle of rebirth.

I am not immortal, and thus
I love with all my heart.
I tend to the garden because
Growth is me playing my part.

I see the tree where the apple hangs.
I see the future and who we became.
I did it for you, and I would do it again.
Seeking the truth is the path of humans.

You say destruction takes one bite, yet
When I open my eyes all I see is white light.
Innovation and complexity wash over the night.
We are not immortal, and thus we must not fight.

Alas, my dear wanderer,
Live by our prayers.
Our spirits reside by the horizon.
One day, I will meet you there . . .

STAGNATION IS DEATH

"Stagnation is death," he said. "Stagnation is death!"
So, I ran to the graveyard with a shovel in hand,
And I dug up all of those who had no chance —
Who knew nothing more than the four
Walls around them and
The ideas they learned, but never tested.

I looked around and I realised almost the entire
Graveyard was excavated.

On the highest ground, with rain pouring and owls
Mourning, I proclaimed,
"Stagnation is death! Take back your life!"
And those bones began to quake.
The earth began to shake.
Those bodies began to wake.

We had an army of vigilance and a mindful set of
Brilliance.
We planted seeds of determination and yeah,
We got our hands dirty in the process.

Turning the soil over, we watered these new ideas.
We could see a difference being made!

The orphan began to shout, "Stagnation is death!"
The mother began to shout, "Stagnation is death!"
The philosopher began to shout. The top leaders
Began to shout.
The trees began to shout. The oceans began to shout.
The world began to shout.

And in a society first built so only the
Privileged could rise —
In a society first built so not everyone could thrive . . .
A shift was heard around the world.
The world was shouting, but not everyone was shouting.

But, then the poor man began to rise,
And the oppressed man began to rise,
And the sister began to rise,
And the believer began to rise . . .
And the man at the very top finally opened his

Pale

Blue

Eyes

And

He

Was

Mesmerised.

WHERE ARE YOUR WINGS?

Ashes to ashes and dust to soul —
We are all a part of the Mother.
A shared fate and a radiant consciousness.

I hear whispers of a muted delight.
A curly, coil-y braid of time is always so refined.
I am a mesa, and the sun gods bless me.

Dear sun sister, shine sweet soliloquies proudly, please.
The earth is my home and the fullness
Thereof.

Though, this constant othering
Is troubling. Can you see the light?
Do you see the might in me, and we?

Ashes to ashes and dust to soul —
We are all a part of one another.
A shared fate and a radiant consciousness.

I hear voices of a shared plight.
I hear voices of a shared spite.
I hear voices of a shared right to live.

A curly, coil-y braid of time is always so refined.
I am a mesa, and the sun gods bless me.
Dear sun brother, sing deep symphonies purely, please.

Wings so white,
We alight on an adventure
To the Earth.

Fallen angel.

Fallen angel.

Now a devil.

Now a rebel.

Where are your wings?

LOVE IS PATIENT

Love is patient and
Love is kind, but
Unlike many things
Love cannot only exist in the mind.

Like striking gold, the river flows
And cannot be stopped

From just being told
Or just turning cold.

How did we get here?
And what can we do?
I am grateful to God
For each and every one of you.

Love is patient and
Love is kind, but
Unlike manmade things

This love is a gift in a realm with no time.

Why does it overwhelm me?
How can I use words to tell thee?
Fumbling to dig deep and feel . . .
It took me a moment to reconcile.

Venus, you open our hearts
When we least expect it
And we are not sure what to do.
We may have no clue which path is true . . .

But, I have a feeling

All roads lead back

To you.

THOUGHTS ON ETERNITY

I found a grey hair today
And it reminded me
Of all the wisdom I have gathered
And my thoughts on eternity.

Well, this body will grow old
And, I will have a million stories told.
Yes, this body will grow old
And what will live on is my eternal soul.

Many lives.

Many timelines.

Many paths unfold . . .

You are safe here.
I hope we believe it.
I hope we feel it.
I hope we mean it.

HOW TO BE WITH SPACE & TIME

Have you ever gotten to a point and a place
Where nothing is on your mind?
I mean absolutely nothing except

The mountains around you,
The river before you,
The wind on your face.

The stones beneath your feet,
The sun's warm embrace.
The patient tree with breath to share,

The moss and leaves and fern and air.
What does it give to be at peace?

Your house, your home, your walls, your fears,

All constructed out of tears.
The human race has turned into battle.
Better, stronger, richer, taller, faster, further — Was this
meant for us?

I ask you,
Have you ever gotten to a point and a place
Where no one is on your mind?

Come with me,
I will show you,
How to be with space and time.

I DID NOT GIVE UP ON YOU

Eva dances in the moonlight with her violin on her chin.
Enchanting, her magic envelopes me.
Fascinating, she taps into the eternal frequency.
I will watch her forever, by her side forever, into eternity.

I did not give up on you
Because that would be giving up on the truth,
And ultimately, I rebuke the slithering roots.
Yes, the misused souls, the broke and loose,
We must rebuke.

Yes, Eva dances in the moonlight with her violin
On her chin.
The uncertainty of life is like a spiral down
A thorny ravine.
Yet, life is so divine.
Yet, life is so divine.

I did not give up on you.

I did not give up on you.

DISCOVERING YOU

Here in Eden there are many words
We are creating and birthing.
What is this feeling with no name?
A warm, grounded essence I cannot contain.

It sways with the breeze in the trees.
It flows like the waves at the sea.
I watch you grow, and I grow too.
I watch you explore, and I am discovering you.

Here in Eden there are many words
We are creating and birthing.
This is something new. All I can say is,
I love you.

YOU ARE SKY BLUE

I knew it once I met you.
Your heart was pure and true.
You smiled with the divine essence.
You held space. You have a presence.

Your radiance blesses my soul.

Lover, lover — Where have you been?
Our paths are shared, and yet within
I know we will grow together.
We will unfold the mysteries of life forever.

Sister, sister.
Mother, mother.
Healer, healer.
Believer, believer.

Bless your heart — Amen.

Four Eyes . . . and three, from Eve.
By the sea — Do not look for me.
In the river — My heart is pure.
I will not let the external affect the internal.

I will not let the past inferno affect the crescendo
Of this love.
I see you everywhere.
I feel you everywhere.

By my side and in our hearts.
You are the light we seek.
I am the beam to meet
You along the path of

Destiny.

You are so beautiful to me.
You are so magnetic to me.
You are one plus one equals three.
To Eve, from Adam.

You changed our lives forever.
You see, I felt your love and energy from
Across the land and seas.

The universe knew I had to be there with thee.

I am in awe of you. I am so proud of you.
If you only knew.
If you only knew. You are so loved. I love you too.
I really do.
I really do.
Because you are sky blue.

You

Are

Sky

Blue.

PETALS ON A WHISPER

She paints petals on a whisper amongst the clouds,
But, the rain is glassy, and the sky is grey.
He practised ministry through technology.
Intercession over time.

Did he minister to all, or did he notice she lost faith?
Well, sometimes I wander where you are.
And sometimes I wonder where you are.

Worn out from the sun . . .

In the forest
Burn the incense
There is more to you!

Climb the mountain
Bring your offering
There is more to lose!

So, get off that Carousel,
Round and round we go.

The game of life is not over and

It is time to ignite our souls.

Yes, I went into the wilderness to find peace.
And all the while,
It was inside of you . . . and me.

IN THE GARDEN OF EDEN

I woke up in a garden.
My hair was full of flowers
And the sun shone bright.

The grass was green.
The scene serene,
But, I could not enjoy it.

I simply could not

Enjoy it.

Because,
I am made
Of stone.

Another beautiful statue,
Alone,
In the garden
Of Eden.

WIND

BE FREE

I meet a monk,
Adorned in red and orange.
I shake her hand and I say,
"What do you see?"
She says,
"Me."
"No, really — What do you see?"
She says,
"Me."
"Okay — What else do you see?"
She says,
"Being free."

THE OTHER SIDE OF THE MOON

Sometimes life rolls
Like tumbleweed —
The wind blows with no meaning.

Then, I bathe in eternal love.
I open my heart.
I am trying to do my part.

Trust me — I am trying to do my part.
My heart holds space for one.
His love is like the shining sun.

May the universe protect you.
May you only know peace.
May the skies never forget you.

May you find a divine release.
May you open your mind to love.
May you respect all paths.

May we make no assumptions
And communicate in a way that makes
Relationships last.
May we go with courage.

May we walk in grace.
May we always hold on to faith.
May our words hold integrity.

May we see the truth.
May we honour our neighbour.
And cherish our youth.

Until next time . . .
Please, continue to

Fly!

Fly!

Fly.

Go with the Divine.
May She walk by your side.
See you next time.

See you soon.
I will certainly see you

On the other side
Of the moon.

AWARE OF IT

Hold onto your happiness.
Hold onto your bliss.
Hold onto your identity.
The deep parts that make you aware of it.

I will always accept you.
I will always listen.
Your jubilance is infectious.
Please take care of it.

Your powers are unconscious
And there is much I must show you.
This is only the beginning,
And there are many things unfolding before you.

Hold onto your happiness.
Hold onto your bliss.
There are moments soon to come,
Where you might not remember it.

TO SWING OR NOT TO SWING?

Wake me up from my winter sublime.

I left all my books behind today and walked to the park
With a friend.
I left all my books, anxieties, concerns, behind today,
And I walked to a nearby park with a friend, and
Sat on a swing set — a seat fit for a Juliet.
To swing or not to swing?
We swung. Two adults thawed by the world around us.
Cars drove by. People walked by. Time went by. But, we
Continued laughing and pumping our feet,
Swinging higher towards the light blue sky, horizontal
And vertical at the same time.
Half hopes of landing in a universe unfazed by
regrets . . .
The air is crisp today and the physics of a swing set bind
Our souls together.

We could say how we felt, but silence often brings
Better explanations.

This bliss will soon pass, and I will walk back to
Unresolved anticipations.

But, there is something about swinging on a swing set
In the sun that brings but innocent peace.

FEEL EMPOWERED
TO CONTROL YOUR LIFE

Oh say,
Can you see?

See what is real and
What is meant to be?

See where there is filth or
Backwards mentality?

See today with all its grace
And stare fear right in the face?

Oh say,
Can you see?

Really, see.

See him and her,
And you and me . . .

I hope you feel empowered to control your life.
I hope you feel empowered to control your life.

Hold on, cara — Stay true, bellezza

PEACE BE UPON US

I pray for peace
So we can save
The human race.

I pray for peace,
Inside of you,
And inside of me.

I pray for peace.
I pray for peace.
I pray for peace!

As-salamu alaykum.
Peace be upon us.
Ah-men.

DOVES IN THE SKY

Western gals steal my song.
Replicate,
Imitate,
Cannot be replicated.

Western boys steal my song.
Relocate,
Navigate,
Safe. Cannot be located.

Doves in the sky.
Keep getting by.
Keep breathing — Now, sigh.

Doves in the sky.
Do not look sideways
Because it is time to fly.

Away,
Away,
Away!

I HAVE SO MUCH LOVE TO GIVE

I crave something I can call
Home.
Someone I can hold onto
And not let go.

I want to see the world.
And hold it tight,
While it holds me,
All through the night.

It says,
"Look!
All that is left is light!
All that is left is light!"

And I proclaim,
"Right!

I have so much love to give!
I have so much love to give!"

MIRRORS

Looking glass
I cannot look past
My soul.

What I see
Only exists
Deep down below.

Mirror cracks,
I collapse —
A curse!

Looking glass
We cannot look past
Our souls.

REIGNITE OUR SOULS

I let you go.
I want you to be free.
I want you to dig deep.
I want you to release

All of your fears
And pain;
All of your anger
And disdain.

And, if it is right,
(And I am sure it might be)
I want you to feel free to
Come back to me.

But, until then,
I say farewell dear friend.

It is time
To reignite
Our Souls.

RELAY THE TRUTH

How are you feeling today?
I am okay. In fact, I cannot say. I feel dread.

What is going on in your head?
So many things, like a rubber balloon filled up with lead.

Can you pop the balloon and reason with your demons?
What do they want from me? They never answer clearly.

One, two, three. May you breathe with me?
What do they want from me? They never answer clearly.

I cannot say, but only I can relay the truth without delay.
I cannot say, but only I can relay my truth avoiding this
heavy dismay.

FIRE

LA GRANDE BELLEZZA

Even the mighty sun
Must slip below the horizon.
Each day we pray
At sunset where we know
Sweet rest is soon knocking at our door.

For now, let us explore one another.
If we went too fast,
I literally might have passed out
From how much I love you.
It is true. It is oddly true.

I love you, Romeo.
It took me by surprise,
But, I do.
I remember the exact moment I met you,
And the deep knowing I felt.

I melted into the present moment.
"Wow," I thought to myself.
"This is the man who will show me how
To save myself."

"Wow," I thought to myself.

"I am the woman who will show him
Beautiful souls are out there, and
Some souls will always truly care
For the other."
Yeah, that is love and

That is life.
I never thought I would find myself there, and
I never thought I would find myself here.
But, I would not have it any other way
Because this is exactly what I prayed for.

You are my number four.

This time, I am sure.

Yin Yang — I will never again leave you standing
Outside in the pouring rain with your heart
In your hands because you
Are also
My dearest friend.

I trust me and thus
I trust you too.
Our energies match — In fact,

When we come into contact,
The particles all explode,

And we unfold into unity.
Yes, that is beauty.
La grande bellezza —
La vita è bella
I'll tell ya . . .

THE MASK

Each morning, I paint on a mask.
Delicate lines of tact:

Elegant

Polite

Muted

Concise

Bubbly

Motherly

Sexy

Lovable

Mystery.

It is all
Exhausting.
A recurring cacophony.

I go to bed
To wake up again
And paint on a mask.

STARS WALTZ

I look outside the window in disbelief.
The world has vanished,
And all that is left is me
And darkness.

Is this a backwards paradise, or
The rise of light's decline?

Must I first be alone
To feel consoled?

I sink beneath the silver waves of an evening bath.
I summon the fires, a sorceress.

Candlelight dances and
Stars waltz.

Can I conjure one person
To fill the time, space, and void?

A resounding no from the universe says,
"Face yourself and be reborn. The soul knows no fear."

I look outside the window in disbelief.
The world has vanished,
And all that is left is me
And the fiery vastness of life.

AN ANGEL

An angel showed up outside my window
Shining bright and white.
I closed the curtains.
So used to darkness and the night,
I was not ready for immanence.

An angel showed up outside my window
Shining bright and white.
I closed the curtains.
Too light — Too bright,
I was not ready for brilliance.

An angel showed up outside my window
Shining bright and white and
I opened those curtains!
Ready to step into my spiritual inheritance,
I was finally ready for personal transcendence.

YOU ARE GOLD

Those who can see life only for what is in front of them
Are dangerous.
And those who can analyse life only in terms of what
Could have been
Are just as dangerous.

But, those who can take a compilation of the
Foreground
And the background
And make life art . . .
Well, those individuals are hard to find,

And those individuals are gold.

Come out of hiding — We need you.

THE BELLIGERENT

A fragile woman in all black hanging by a thread
Will always look to steal
Your security.

And if she cannot steal it from you,
She will try desperately to
Cast a web and poison your stew.

Simmer, simmer, bubble, spittle.
A potion meant to make you little.
Simmer, simmer, bubble, dribble.
A motion meant to start a quibble.

Only with a counter dance will you stand a chance!
The anecdote is indifference.
Make her recognize her insignificance.

Because your precious energy is magnificent.
We only spar with equivalents.
It is only fair against the belligerent.

LET GO

Let go or be dragged.
It is too expensive if
It costs you your peace or your happiness.

Ikigai, find your purpose.
Give back and do not resist.
The theatre of dreams says, "Play!"

So, play. We are not here forever.
We may not be here tomorrow.
So do it all the way with no regrets!

Speak life into your dreams because
We have this one chance.
Each and every choice will make a difference.

DON'T YOU DARE, JUDAS

"Judas.
Hey, Judas!
Is that you?"

A wolf in sheep's clothing
Stands before me
In white.

"Judas.
Hey, Judas!
Is that you?"

Do not be deceived.
His new look is contrived
From conceit.

"Judas.
Hey, Judas!
I know it is you!

Do not dare
To bring your filth and despair
Into this town!"

I chase him in a fit of tears.

"Do not dare
To bring your filth and despair
Into our town!"

DRY RIVER

I am a supernova.
I fly high
Through the sky, and I am
Fiery and indulgent.

To dance amongst the stars
Is an honour fit for the Gods.
Dark and bright
I ignite my truth.

But, at the very root
I cannot compute
What we have done to
The lands we say we love.

When did the waters turn brown?
When did the rivers run dry?
When did the crops turn foul?
When did the children not cry?

What have you done, my beloved,
To the luscious land I gave?
What have you done my beloved?
Do you not understand everything we
Could have made?

Go down to the river and
Begin to shed your tears.
Stay there weeping patiently
So the streams can be refilled after all these years.

TESTIFY

"I am ready to testify!" she says, hobbling her way
to the altar.

Yes, sister, testify! Let the Lord's fire burn!

"I cannot lie. God is good. He is so good. He brought
my husband and I our second son. He is here in my
stomach. He brought him after all He promised."

Yes sister, after all your prayers!

"Thank you, Jesus."

He will never leave us.

Testify, testify!

Justify your sins!

Tithe away your wins!

The Lord is returning . . . soon!

WATER

AVALANCHE — WATERFALL

Avalanche,
Waterfall.

Lost my chance,
Had to fall.

Happenstance,
Logical.

Circumstance,
Magical.

Take a chance and
Watch it all

Avalanche,
Waterfall.

MOUNT ARARAT & MY COVENANT

Rest your ship on Mount Ararat. Once the floods
Subside, the birds will sing.
You have fulfilled a divine prophecy
And only a few can accompany me
To our new world. Though, I did not
Spare the aristocracy,
Or those who tout a lofty legacy.
I spared the humble, the open minded,
And the aware. I did not spare
The man with the most words or the finest hair.
I spared the honest, the marginalised,
And the morally fair.

This rainbow is my covenant.

This

Rainbow

Is

My covenant.

It is the promise I always meant
To give you and to show you.
It is the promise I always meant
For you.
I hope you always think of it when
Clouds start to form, and you feel a pull
To conform. You are so much more!

This is my covenant.

A WEB OF TIME

I am nice to her, but
She is mean back.
She felt the pain
Our father could not.
You see, crucifixion leaks
A poison in our DNA.
Constant martyrs and
Unconscious mothers . . .
We are caught in a web
Of time.

I am nice to her, but
She is mean back.
Feeling a deep lack always
Puts us on the
Wrong track.
You see, I still have
Your back.
Yeah, I have your back.
We are simply caught in a web
Of time.

SUNSHINE ON THE WAY

Yesterday, it was sunny.
I danced and laughed and sang.
If I knew what was coming,
I would have held on to yesterday.

Today, I stood in a storm.
The trees howled and I was tossed.
I sunk into a deep hole to drown.
The rain was pouring in from overhead.

Tomorrow makes me nervous.
Will it be sun or rain or snow?
I know I should be patient
And grateful for a soul at all.

Yesterday, today, tomorrow . . .
Some days I cannot bear it.
If I carry on another day, it is okay!
There must be sunshine on the way.

What do you believe in?

BENEATH THE TIDE

The grass is greener
Always leaner
On the other side.

Then assumptions make
Brash abrasions when
Expectations collide.

I can never stand
The weather when clouds
Cover our eyes.

I can never understand
The measure of our shared
And disappearing times.

The grass is greener
Always leaner
On the other side.

Do not forget, it is
Not always what you expect
Beneath the tide.

LET MY PEOPLE GO

Servants to whom and what?
We build false gods and heed false prophets.

We chase the pharaoh
Wherever the wind blows.
Saying His name in vain, we cannot sustain it all.

We are simply lost in thought!
I suppose we cannot control our wants.

We are simply lost in thought!
I suppose we cannot control our faults.

Yet still here I cry from
Deep in my belly,
"Let my people go!"

FAST THROUGH THE MUD

I thought I lost everything,
And then I woke up and realised
There was more to lose.

Fresh out of luck and I was stuck.

I thought I could handle anything
And then you set the dogs loose.
I ran so fast through the mud. I had no clue.

Fresh out of luck and I was stuck.

I thought I caught a break.
I opened the gift box and inside
There was a silver and emerald snake.

Fresh out of luck and I was stuck.

I gave up. I surrendered.
The sun cannot and will not shine
Up north in November.

DRENCHED IN SALT

We shared this bed for years. I thought we were on the same page. I thought we were in the same world. As things unfold, I realise, I did not know you at all.

The walls began to fall and my world
tumbled into the sea.

"Help me! I cannot be swept away to sea. It scares me.
Help me! I fear loneliness and strife and depravity.
Help me! I did not plan for such a calamity."

A grand hand scooped me from the waves. "My dear, why are you drenched in salt and pain?" Dried and with fresh clothes, he put me back in bed.

We shared this bed for years. I thought we were on the same page. I thought we were in the same world. As things unfold, I realise, I did not own you at all.

LIFE IS THE TASTE OF HONEY

Perfect peace in
A precious sanctuary
Conceals the truth.

The River Nile —
In a wooden canoe.
Unlock your roots.

Buzzing bees —
Taste the honey.
Then, put on your boots.

By the sea —
Do not look for me.
There is more to do!

In the forest —
Burn the incense.
There is more to you!

Climb the mountain and
Bring your offering.
There is always more to lose!

The world is always bigger than we think.
It is full of people with their unique stories.
It is full of magic, mystery, and glory.
If you have the chance, make plans for discovery.

The things you will uncover can change your life
Forever.